L

IS EN

ON
ARCHITECTURE
AND
ASCETICISM

This essay is dedicated to the memory of
Giuseppe Dossetti (1913–1996).

PIER VITTORIO AURELI

CONTENTS

INTRODUCTION

For many years, 'less is more' has been the catch-phrase of minimalist design. Instantly associated with the restrained work of the German architect Ludwig Mies van der Rohe, who borrowed this dictum from a poem by Robert Browning,[1] 'less is more' celebrates the ethical and aesthetic value of a self-imposed economy of means. Mies's stripped-bare architecture, in which formal expression was reduced to a simple composition of readymade industrial elements, implied that beauty could only arise through refusal of everything that was not strictly necessary. In recent years, but especially since the 2008 economic recession, the 'less is more' attitude has become fashionable again, this time advocated by critics, architects and designers in a slightly moralistic tone.[2]

If in the late 1990s and early 2000s architecture was driven by the irrational exuberance of the real-estate market towards the production of increasingly redundant iconic objects, with the onset of the recession the situation started to change. Those who had previously acclaimed (or even produced) the acrobatics of architecture in the previous decade now took to complaining about architecture's shameful waste of resources and budgets.[3] This change of sensibility has provoked two kinds of reaction. Some architects have tried to translate the ethos of austerity in merely formal terms.[4] Others have advocated a more socially minded approach, trying to go beyond the traditional boundaries of architecture.[5] It would be unfair to put these positions on the same level (as the second may be more plausible than the first), but what they seem to share is the idea that the current crisis is an opportunity to do—as an Italian architect turned politician put it—'more with less'.[6] It is for this reason that 'less is more' is no longer just an aesthetic principle but the kernel of the ideology of something else, something where economy of means is not just a design strategy but an economic imperative *tout court*.

Within the history of capitalism, 'less is more' defines the advantages of reducing the costs of production. Capitalists have always tried to obtain *more* with *less*. Capitalism is not just a process of accumulation but also, and especially, the incessant optimisation of the productive process towards a situation in which *less* capital investment equals more capital accumulation. Technological innovation has always been driven by the imperative to reduce the costs of production, the need for wage earners. The very notion of *industry* is based on this idea: to be *industrious* means being able to obtain the best results with fewer means.[7] Here we see how creativity itself is at the very root of the notion of industry. Creativity depends not just on the investor finding ways to spare resources but on the worker's capacity to adapt to difficult situations. These two aspects of industriousness and creativity are interlinked: the worker's creativity forcibly becomes more pronounced when capital decides to reduce the costs of production and economic conditions become uncertain. Indeed it is creativity, as the most generic faculty of human life, that capital has always exploited as its main labour power. And in an economic crisis, what capital's austerity measures demand is that people do more with less: more work for less money, more creativity with less social security. In this context, the principle of 'less is more' runs the risk of becoming a cynical celebration of the ethos of austerity and budget cuts to social programmes.

In what follows I would like to address the condition of *less* not by rejecting it but by critically assessing its ambiguity. Both the 'less is more' attitude in design and the ethos of austerity politics seem to converge within the tradition of asceticism, which is commonly understood as a practice of abstinence from worldly pleasures. In recent years asceticism has indeed been identified as the source, both ideological and moral, of the idea of austerity.[8] A major argument put forward in favour of cutting public spending is that we have been living beyond our means and that from now on we will have to lower our expectations of future wealth and social security. Only by making 'sacrifices' will we find the path to salvation and avoid economic armageddon. In an economy driven by public debt asceticism has a particular resonance, in the form of moral guilt. Debt is not only about economy but is first and foremost a moral contract between creditor and debtor. As Maurizio Lazzarato has recently argued, the neoliberal economy is a subjective economy that is no longer based—as classical economics was—on the producer and the barterer.[9] A fundamental figure of the neoliberal economy is the 'indebted man'—that is, the indebted consumer, the indebted user of the welfare state and, in the case of nation state debt, the indebted citizen. To be indebted does not only mean owing something to someone; it is also the feeling of guilt, and thus of inferiority, towards the creditor. It is precisely the subject's sense of guilt and longing for atonement that is often understood to constitute the meaning of ascetic practices.

Asceticism is here understood as abstinence and self-discipline, as a willingness to sacrifice our present in order to earn our future—something which goes beyond the religious meaning of the term and has more to do with the ethics of entrepreneurial capitalism. In his famous book, *The Protestant Ethic and the Spirit of Capitalism*, Max Weber identifies two kind of asceticism: *inner-worldly* and *other-worldly*.[10] In the first instance, asceticism denotes withdrawal from the world, as in the case of hermits and monks; in the second case, asceticism becomes more secular and addresses the possibility of an existence that frees itself from mundane distractions in order to dedicate itself fully to the ethics of work and production. Weber sees other-worldly asceticism as one of the fundamental sources of the ethics of capitalism: with the advent of Calvinism, he notes, asceticism spread beyond the confines of the monastery and became a diffuse mentality within the city. Asceticism required the repression of natural instincts and adherence to a strict discipline of ethical rationality. For Weber this ethical rationality was both the foundation of the bourgeois life-style and the very 'spirit' of capitalism as later manifested in Benjamin Franklin's economic utilitarianism, which was concerned not only with the rational acquisition of means towards an end, but was in itself a transcendental ethical goal.

Here Weber proposes that asceticism paved the way for a profound transformation of human subjectivity, giving it the capacity to undertake the continual adjustments of the inner self that are required by the economic processes of capitalism, which are never resolved—there is no end in sight, either in terms of satisfying personal needs or even in the mere process of accumulation. Although Weber's argument remains one of the most powerful readings of asceticism, I have chosen a slightly different path in what follows. Precisely because the practice of asceticism addresses the transformation of the self, I argue that it can be both a means of oppression and also a form of resistance to the subjective power of capitalism.

When we talk about resistance to power we understand this concept in terms of ideology or belief, but rarely as a matter of habits, customs and even the most humble aspects of everyday life. What is interesting about asceticism is that it allows subjects to focus on their life as the core of their own practice, by structuring it according to a self-chosen form made of specific habits and rules. This process often involves architecture and design as a device for self-enactment. Because asceticism allows subjects to focus on their *self* as the core of their activity, the architecture that has developed within this practice is an architecture focused not on representation, but on life itself— on *bios*, as the most generic substratum of human existence. As others have argued, the development of modern architecture itself, with its emphasis on issues such as hygiene, comfort and social control, has been driven by a biopolitical logic.[11] However, it is especially within asceticism that the enactment of forms of life becomes explicit. This is evident, for example, within the history of monasticism, where the architecture of the monastery was expressly designed to define life in all its most immanent details. Although monasticism ultimately spawned such disciplinary and repressive typologies as the *Hôtel-Dieu*, the hospital, the garrison, the prison and even the factory, at the outset the main purpose of its asceticism was to achieve a form of reciprocity between subjects freed from the social contract imposed by established forms of power. And this is why this tradition still stands as a paradigm for our time, when capital is becoming not only increasingly repressive but also increasingly unable to 'take care' of its subalterns as it did in the heyday of the welfare state. We will see that asceticism is not the preserve of monks in cells but, on the contrary, suffuses everything from the logic of capitalism itself to the concept of 'social' housing and the ideological rhetoric of minimalist design. The question is, can it lead us towards a different way of life than the one forced upon us by the status quo?

CHAPTER
I

CHAPTER I

The word 'ascetic' comes from the Greek *askein,* which means exercise, self-training. Asceticism is a way of life in which the *self* is the main object of human activity. For this reason the practice of asceticism is not necessarily related to religion. Indeed it is possible to argue that the very first ascetics were philosophers. In ancient times the fundamental goal of philosophy was to know oneself: to live was understood not simply as given fact but as an *art,* the art of living. Within asceticism life becomes *ars vivendi,* something to which it is possible to give a specific form. In the case of the ancient philosophers this meant a life entirely consistent with one's own teachings, where there was no difference between theory and practice, between *logos* and *bios.* Philosophers were thus individuals who, through their chosen form of life, deeply informed by their thinking, inevitably challenged accepted habits and social conditions.[12]

Asceticism is thus not just a contemplative condition, or a withdrawal from the world as it is commonly understood, but is, above all, a way to radically question given social and political conditions in a search for a different way to live one's life. It was for this reason that early Christianity absorbed asceticism, in the form of monasticism. In the process, however, asceticism acquired a very different meaning. Its main goal was no longer to change the existing social order, but rather to

15

prepare for the Second Coming of Christ: it was practised as a precondition for salvation. And yet those who embraced monastic life also did so as a way of refusing the integration of the Christian faith within the institutions of power. The origins of monasticism in the West coincide with the recognition of the Catholic Church by the Roman Emperor Constantine and the beginning of a political and cultural alliance between Church and State. Although this alliance gave the Church immense power, it also eroded its 'underground' identity, which was crucial for its proselytism.[13] For many Christians, the institutionalisation of the Church put it on a path of fatal compromise and decline. Rejecting the new position of ecclesiastical power, the early monks not only chose a life of ascetic solitude (in fact the word monk comes from the Greek *monos*, alone), they also decided to live outside the law and the rights that defined social life. Monastic life began in the deserts of Syria and Egypt, places that gave the early hermits a cultural *tabula rasa* where they could start again from scratch.[14] From the outset, monasticism manifested itself as an inevitable and radical critique of power, not by fighting against it, but by leaving it: the form of life of the monk was to be homeless, to be foreign, to refuse any role within society.[15] While the Church, after its absorption into the apparatuses of state power, was at pains to give itself a strict institutional order, early monasticism manifested itself as the refusal of any institution and as a desire to live an ascetic life freed from social constraints.

In his *Genealogy of Morals*, Nietzsche puts forward a fundamental critique of asceticism, attempting to demonstrate how the desire to refuse the world is not a mere withdrawal, as the hermits and early monks maintained, but a subtle manifestation of man's will to power.[16] In doing so he rediscovers the original meaning of asceticism as control of oneself and, by extension, a necessary precondition for political power over others. Although he is critical of asceticism, he nevertheless understands this practice as paradigmatic of the more general evolution of human subjectivity, a process he calls the *internalising of man*, in which the partial suppression and containment of primitive instincts such as hunting, cruelty, hostility and destruction made it possible for man to exist peacefully within a society. For Nietzsche the ascetic ideal of priesthood, with its hatred for the sensual, is the culmination of this process of internalising instincts, and as such is something to hate. At the same time he (reluctantly) acknowledges that it was precisely this process of self-repression that made humans human.

Asceticism is thus understood by Nietzsche as a radical form of reactive containment through which the human species preserves itself by negating itself, by suppressing its own vital forces. And yet he sees this process of containment not as a reduction of human potential but as the true source of man's will to power. In other words, for Nietzsche the life of asceticism reveals the fundamental datum of human existence that is the never-resolved tension between *desire* and *restraint*, where neither prevails over the other but both coexist in a constant precarious equilibrium. Monasticism and the forms of life that it engenders carry this aspect of human nature to its ultimate limit.

CHAPTER
II

Monasticism has evolved through different forms, from the eremitic life of solitude away from communities; to the semi-eremitic, where hermits live together in an unprescribed way; to the cenobitic, in which the monks not only live in the same place but also share the same monastic rule. The early monks who decided to live together would occupy single huts loosely aggregated around a central space, which in many cases would be the church. As Roland Barthes has remarked, this condition allowed the monks to live together but apart, with each being able to preserve, as he put it, their own 'idiorrhythmy' (from the Greek *idios*, particular and *rhythmos*, rhythm, rule).[17] In this condition they would be both isolated from and in contact with one another, in idiorrhythmic clusters. Within the clusters, living together did not wholly impinge on the possibility of being alone. Barthes was fascinated by this way of living, and noted that precisely this form of monasticism was the seedbed for what would later become a fundamental typology of the modern world: the single cell or single room. For Barthes the single cell is the quintessential representation of interiority: it is here that the single body finds its proper space, the space in which it can take care of itself.

The idea of a structure where individual and collective life are juxtaposed without being merged is also evident in Carthusian monasticism, which attempted to combine eremitic and cenobitic life in the same place. One of the most remarkable examples of this tradition is the Monastery of Galluzzo, near Florence, which had a strong influence on Le Corbusier's idea of collective housing. In this monastery, the cloister binds together nine distinct houses, each of them equipped with a garden and basic facilities for individual living. The architecture is modest and austere, but the possibility of individual seclusion supported by the necessary equipment to live alone gives these lilliputian houses an air of luxury. Luxury not in the sense of possession: there is nothing to possess here apart from a few books and the food necessary to survive. Rather, in these houses, luxury is the possibility for the inhabitants to live according to their own proper rhythm.

Aside from the duties of contemplation and silence, we have to understand that such a life could represent a fundamental liberation from a social structure that was very repressive towards individual life. Within the Carthusian monastery, the houses were accessible from the main cloister, which also gave access to the communal facilities. In this way the individual houses were not fully independent but were completed by more collective programmes. The concentration of collective facilities allowed the individual houses to be minimal spaces for living.

The balance between individual and collective life is the fundamental issue within monastic life, as became clear with the rise of the cenobitic monastery, when communal life became the dominant way of living. Initiated by the Coptic monk Pachomius, perfected by St Benedict, and radically reformed by St Francis, the common life of the cenobium can only be experienced through the sharing of a rule.[18]

Like performing arts such as acting and dance, monasticism is an art that does not leave behind a product but coincides with the performance itself. Within cenobitic monasticism, life is formalised in minute detail. From the clothes, to the cell, to the daily rhythm of prayers and work, nothing is left to chance. Not only specific moments, but all actions, even the most simple daily routines, are ritualised as an incessant *opus dei*. The cenobitic monastery provides us with the first instance of the management of time through strict scheduling. Bells give the hours a specific sound (which we can still hear in many Western cities), which regulates the sequence of activities with the same precision as a Taylorist factory. The body of the monk is also strictly regulated. The very idea of the habit, which describes both a personal attitude and a collective ethos, becomes within monasticism a specific object, the *habitus*, the clothing worn by monks and prelates.

And yet what is meant above all to condition the life of the monks is the architecture of the monastery. Within the monastery, form follows function in the strictest way possible. Like a functionalist building, the typical form of the medieval monastery is simply an extrusion of the ritual activities that take place within. If we observe the plan of the monastery we see a perfect coincidence of time and space: each segment of the day is ritualised through a specific activity that takes place in a specific part of the monastery. The introverted space of the cloister, the point of access to most of the facilities, gives a precise form to communal life and the sense of sharing, while the simple unobstructed rectangular plan of the chapterhouse defines the gathering together of the monks in the most essential way. The dormitories are large rooms divided into cubicles by fabric. The cubicles offer a measure of privacy but at the same time the light materiality of the walls, which can be removed, is a reminder that individual space is always the sharing of a larger collective space.[19]

Rather than a generic container or a symbolic monument, the architecture of the monastery is an apparatus that obsessively frames and identifies living activities. It is not by chance that the first known architectural drawing is the famous plan most probably drafted as a blueprint for an 'ideal' Benedictine monastery, preserved in the library of the Monastery of St Gallen. The plan is rendered as a series of clearly enclosed spaces defined through the activity that these spaces are meant to contain.

The plan of the monastery suggests an architecture that is conceived to be completely self-sufficient, and self-sufficiency is central to the communal life. The monastery shows in clear terms that a truly communitarian life can only be achieved through a consistent organisation of time and space. This is the most controversial aspect of the monastery, because it shows how this institution is the progenitor of disciplinary institutions such as the prison, the garrison, the hospital and the factory. Moreover, it is not difficult to see how the scheduling of time and its management are the foundation of modern and contemporary forms of production.[20] And yet the difference between the ascetic practices enacted by the monastery and the disciplinary power of these other institutions is as subtle as it is decisive. The strict organisation of the monastery was not intended to replace life with a rule, but to make the rule so consistent with the form of life chosen by the monks that the rule as such would almost disappear.[21] This aspect of monasticism is made evident in the simplest monastic rule ever presented, which is the one drafted by Augustine: *dilige et quod vis fac*—love and do what you want. Unlike the logic of disciplinary institutions, the *ends* here do not justify the *means*; rather, means and ends perfectly coincide. What Augustine emphasised as the goal of monastic life was the practice of unconditional love for one's neighbour, that is, a radical form of fraternal reciprocity where no one prevails over the other. Through a return to the ascetic principles of early monasticism, mendicant orders such as the Cistercians and the Franciscans would radically reform monastic life, opposing the entrepreneurialism and ethos of production that plagued the Benedictine tradition. As has been noted, this reform gave rise to one of the most radical experiments in living, one that was completely antithetical to the principle that has regulated modern forms of power, namely the concept of private property.

CHAPTER
III

Benedictine monasteries were highly productive, becoming centres of power and wealth to the point where the order's most famous monastery, Cluny, expanded into a city in its own right. Against this, the early Franciscans openly rejected the idea of private property, meaning not just individual possessions but, above all, the possibility of owning the work of others—of owning potential *capital*, in the form of land or tools. The desire to secure ownership of something is motivated not just by its use but by its potential to become an economic asset, to generate profit. If one refuses ownership of something one can still use it without possessing it. The concept of use, in this sense, is the antithesis of the concept of private property.

A fundamental tenet of the early Franciscan order was indeed the refusal to own things, as a way of refusing their potential economic value and thus the possibility of exploiting others. Rather than owning a robe, a house or a book, they would *use* these things. Here use was understood not as a value but as the act of sharing things, as the supreme form of living in *common*. Use implied the temporary appropriation of an object by an individual; after its use, the object would be released and thus shared with others. In its simplicity, this conception of use implied a radical *abdicatio iuris*, given that the whole modern conception of rights is fundamentally shaped by the individual's right to private property. The Franciscan concept of *altissima paupertas* (poverty as a self-imposed and thus desired form of life) was inspired by the life of animals, in which the concept of ownership does not exist.[22] The early Franciscans proposed a radical experiment: a form of life devoid of private property, in which coexistence and sharing would become the main object of an ascetic practice. Their *experimentum vitae* was short-lived, because the Church forced them to renounce it after a subtle but intense judicial dispute, and yet this failure reveals how private property—the very thing that the Franciscans wanted at all costs to avoid—had become the defining aspect of the modern way of living. The meaning of asceticism changed. With the rise of property as a fundamental social asset, it was no longer a self-chosen practice, but more an ethical and moral condition whose goal was to ensure social control and increase dedication to work. Private property and its accumulation became not simply a means of power, but a sort of transcendental instigation for people to become more focused, and thus dependent, on their economic condition.

CHAPTER
IV

The historical evolution of the modern city is unthinkable without the concept of private property. With the decline of feudalism, people acquired individual rights thanks to the rise of economic entrepreneurialism. In the reborn cities of the Middle Ages, owning private property was a precondition for citizenship. In this way, individual ownership became the foundation of modern political institutions. The house was no longer just a shelter, or the ancient *oikos*, the private household clearly separated from public space. It was now both a space of inhabitation and the economic and legal apparatus through which the rising modern state governed citizens by defining their most intimate conditions, that is their habits, customs and social and economic relationships. From the vantage point of governing institutions, property in the form of housing serves a two-fold purpose. On the one hand, it binds the individual to a place and thus reduces the risks of social deviance. On the other, it allows subjects to use their minimum possession as an economic asset, with the capacity for investment. This is why housing became a fundamental project for modern architecture, a project focused not only on sheltering individuals but on making household management productive.

It was in the early modern period that rental housing started to become a diffuse practice within the city. Houses were built not only to shelter the family or the clan, but also to be rented to people outside the boundaries of kinship. The sixteenth-century architect Sebastiano Serlio devoted one of his seven books on architecture to houses.[23] What is novel about Serlio's treatise is its focus on the design of houses for all classes. For the first time in history, even the houses of the peasant and the artisan are considered as a design problem. For these subjects Serlio proposes a minimum dwelling unit which clearly reflects the ascetic character of the inhabitant. But here asceticism is not the inhabitant's choice. Serlio's little house is not for the hermit, or for those who have consciously chosen to reject private property. The poverty embodied by Serlio's minimal house is a 'productive' poverty because it makes living conditions for the poor a little more bearable, so enabling them to reproduce their labour and to become productive subjects, 'workers'. Here the ascetic restraint of architecture, which has characterised the evolution of modern 'social' housing from Serlio's house onwards, represents the ethos of sacrifice and hard work for the sake of production. And yet what is interesting is that Serlio applies the same restraint to his models of houses for professionals such as merchants, lawyers and clerks. Unlike his predecessors, who designed architecture only for popes, princes and cardinals, Serlio addresses society at large. Influenced by protestant evangelism, Serlio was what today we would call a 'socially minded architect', a designer who was not afraid to abandon the monumental form of architecture in favour of social amelioration. But for all of its good intentions, this tendency frequently reveals the most problematic aspects of architecture as a patronising apparatus.

Perhaps the best embodiment of this model for dwelling is Le Corbusier's Maison Dom-Ino (1914), a simple structural concrete framework that could be built by the inhabitants themselves with minimal resources and filled in according to their means.[24] And yet, the very goal of the Dom-Ino model was to provide the lower classes with a minimum property that would allow them to become entrepreneurs of their own household condition. This same principle has been applied on a mass scale in the development of many Mediterranean cities since the postwar period, most notably Athens and Rome. Here the possibility of ownership has been extended to all classes, especially the lower classes, by tacitly encouraging the small-scale building industry. The goal of these economic processes is to form a society of owners where even the smallest, seemingly most worthless property is seized as an opportunity for financial investment.

All of these examples illustrate the paradoxical marriage between asceticism and property. On the one hand subjects are encouraged to endure reduced living standards, and on the other they are pushed to become micro-entrepreneurs of their own minimal economy. This conversion of asceticism into the potential for development is a betrayal of its core principles. As we have seen, asceticism was conceived to allow autonomy from systems of power. It offers the possibility of designing a form of life that challenges established modes of governance. In capitalism, however, asceticism is appropriated as a moral imperative directing the subject to work harder, produce, accumulate and finally consume more. Paradoxically, asceticism becomes a form of life in which sacrifice and hard work are seen as the necessary foundation for future revenue and consumption—or, in times of economic recession, as the sole means to repay a debt. Just as scarcity of resources represents one of the fundamental tropes of capitalism—an exhortation to perform productively by competition and abnegation—asceticism becomes the moral legitimation of the status quo.

CHAPTER
V

CHAPTER V

At the beginning of the 1930s Walter Benjamin wrote several essays in which he attacked nineteenth-century bourgeois interiors.[25] For Benjamin, the bourgeois apartment was filled with objects whose sole purpose was to reaffirm the ideology of the private home. He observed how furniture and interior design were driven not by necessity but by the inhabitants' urge to leave their own traces, that is to make the living space familiar, to claim it as their own. The result was a forced domesticity in which every object was meant to speak of the life of the inhabitants. Benjamin's critique was very subtle because it did not approach the bourgeois interior from a populist anti-consumerist stance. At that moment Europe, and especially Germany, was suffering the fallout of the 1929 crash, and millions of people (including Benjamin himself) were living in precarious conditions. In Berlin in particular, not only the lower classes but also people used to the bourgeois comforts of the Wilhelmine period were suddenly exposed to the fragility of their possessions. The nineteenth-century domestic interior, stripped of its pretence of family stability and economic confidence, was revealed in all its unbearable melancholic anguish. Benjamin understood the subjective dimension of private property, which entails not only greed and appropriation, but also the illusion of permanence, rootedness and identity.

Against this model of inhabitation, Benjamin proposed the possibility of emptiness in the form of a 'tabula rasa', a space devoid of identity, possession or a sense of belonging. His famous essay, 'Experience and Poverty', describes the bare concrete structures designed by Le Corbusier as the incarnation of such architecture.[26] It is ironic that Benjamin associated Corb's minimalism with a radical form of living when, as we have seen, it was meant to enforce the mechanism of property on a even vaster scale than the nineteenth-century bourgeois interior. And yet Le Corbusier's bare architecture was for him the most honest representation of the brutality of the industrialised life: only a domestic space devoid of familiar traces and identity is able to reflect our condition of precarity, the poverty of experience engendered by industrialisation and the wealth of information that pervades life in the metropolis. For Benjamin, poverty of experience does not imply personal poverty, or even abstinence from the abundance of things and ideas that a capitalistic society produces. On the contrary, poverty of experience is precisely the effect of this abundance. Inundated by all sorts of information, stories and beliefs—'the oppressive wealth of ideas that has been spread among people, or rather has swamped them entirely', as Benjamin put it—we can no longer trust the depth and richness of human experience. Living in a context of constant cognitive stimulation, what we experience is no longer effectively communicable. It is for this reason that the only acceptable way of life for Benjamin is to be a modern 'barbarian' who is able to start from nothing and make 'a little go a long way; to begin from little and build up further, looking neither left, nor right'.[27] Here Benjamin introduces one of the most radical and subversive versions of asceticism in modernity, which consists in the act of transforming the most devastating aspects of modern experience, such as uprootedness and precarity, into the emancipating force he defined in one of his most beautiful and enigmatic *denkbilder,* the 'Destructive Character'.[28] It is easy to imagine that Benjamin saw this character as the ethos born out of the unstable situation of Weimar Germany, where the economic crisis, the rise of fascism and conformism gave little hope for the decade to come. But this ethos was also Benjamin's life itself. At 40, he found himself living in a situation of constant uncertainty, working as a freelance critic and changing address frequently (in the 1930s he moved 19 times). Like a medieval mendicant monk, he was determined to turn this ethos of uprootedness into the possibility of starting anew. He invoked the 'Destructive Character' as a liberating force. As he wrote in the most crucial passage of this text:

The destructive character knows only one watchword: make room. And only one activity: clearing away. His need for fresh air and open space is stronger than any hatred.[29]

Here Benjamin seems to be close to one of his beloved heroes: Charles Baudelaire, the poet who made the instability of the modern city not just something to represent but something to live, to experience directly and consciously reconstruct through the craft of one's own life. Refusing to work methodically, Baudelaire made his aimless wandering in the metropolis his very life's work. As Michel Foucault has noted, Baudelaire's favourite characters, such as the flâneur and the dandy, can be understood as manifestations of asceticism in whom life itself is crafted as a work of art. And yet this crafting of one's own life always implies the possibility of self-destruction, which Baudelaire not only evoked in his poems but lived directly, by deliberately embracing a precarious way of life. Baudelaire abhorred traditional apartment dwelling and lived instead in tiny rooms, moving often, mostly because he was chased by his creditors but also because of his hatred of conforming. Like a monk, Baudelaire reduced his personal belongings to a minimum in order to use the city itself as a vast habitation, a place large enough to be adrift.

It is interesting to note that in the same year that he wrote 'Experience and Poverty' and 'The Destructive Character', Benjamin produced another small piece in which he described with sober sympathy the way people lived in Moscow after the 1917 Revolution.[30] Instead of owning their own homes, Muscovites owned rooms, and their possessions were so drastically reduced that they could reinvent their way of inhabiting their own space almost every day. As Benjamin observed, this condition pushed people to dwell in communal spaces such as the club and the street. Benjamin had no utopian illusions about this way of life. Being himself a 'precarious' freelance intellectual worker with no stable income, he knew all too well that to live within a minimally furnished room was more a necessity than a choice. And yet for Benjamin the more this condition was made explicit in the architecture of the interior, the more it would offer the ground for a radical way of living.

Perhaps the best representation of this ideal of living is Hannes Meyer's Co-op Zimmer project, conceived for an exhibition on cooperative design in Ghent in 1924.[31] The design was premised on the idea of a classless society in which every member would own the same minimum. All that remains of this project is a photograph which shows the room as a space defined by two walls formed of fabric. Meyer's room was intended to showcase a way of life in which workers' increasing nomadism and uprootedness would be reflected by an interior that was easy to inhabit. In the Co-op Zimmer furniture is reduced to the minimum necessary for inhabitation by one person: a case, folded chairs that can be hung on the wall, and a single bed. The only 'superfluous' object is a gramophone whose curvy shapes are in contrast with the restrained atmosphere of the room. And yet the gramophone is important because it shows that the minimal living of the Co-op Zimmer is not only dictated by necessity, but is also a space to reclaim an element of 'unproductive' time.

Unlike many architects of his day, Meyer defined the room, rather than the apartment, as the main unit for living, thus avoiding the whole issue of *existenzminimum*, which was concerned with the minimal dimensions of a family house. Meyer's project instead postulates a situation in which the room for one individual implies that collective space is left unrestricted by any standard. Unlike the private house, which is the origin of the real-estate logic of the city, the room is implicitly a space that is never self-sufficient. Like the monastic cell, the Co-op Zimmer is not a form of possession but rather the minimal space that allows each individual person to live by sharing the rest of the dwelling space. Here, privacy is not property, but rather the possibility of solitude and concentration—a possibility that our 'productive' and 'social' lives often tend to eliminate. This idea of positive seclusion is suggested by the sobriety of Meyer's design, which does not glamorise poverty but shows it for what it is. For Meyer, unlike Mies, less is not more, less is just enough. And yet the atmosphere in the Co-op Zimmer is not one of repressive austerity; on the contrary, it suggests a sense of calm and hedonistic enjoyment. Meyer seems to realise the idea of communism as it was defined by Bertolt Brecht: 'the equal distribution of poverty'. Brecht's statement not only mocks the very idea of capitalism as the best way to manage a situation of scarcity but understands poverty as a value, as a desired form of life which can become a luxury, paradoxically, only when it is shared by all. And yet it is here that we also find the great danger of asceticism, which is its mere aestheticisation, as a style, as an atmosphere.

CHAPTER VI

Minimal design has evolved precisely from the transformation of the moral imperative of restraint into an easily recognisable aesthetic. The most obvious example is the architecture of John Pawson, whose minimal design ranges from luxury villas and boutiques to a monastery in Novy Dvur, Czech Republic. Made only of white plastered walls and simple shapes, Pawson's architecture is minimal to the point of inadvertently denouncing itself as cliché. In a hilarious conversation, which is also one the best critiques of minimalist design, a monk living in Pawson's monastery reveals that the commission came about after one of the monks visited the Calvin Klein store in New York, designed by the British architect. Faced with the spectacle of simplicity, the monk was ecstatic: 'It was so pure nothing distracted from the product, it was shopping taken to a religious level. Wouldn't it make a wonderful monastery, we thought, if we replaced Fashion with God?'[32]

Here we see how easy it is to turn asceticism into a disingenuous caricature. Ascetic restraint is easily interchangeable with marketing, especially in times of recession, when there is a rush to embrace the rhetoric of anti-consumerism and the return to core values. As a counter to the phenomenon of 'starchitects'—the architects who participated in the frenzy of architectural spectacle over the last 20 years—many critics invoke the reclusive architect who refuses to participate, who is able to refrain from openly market-driven commissions.

In recent years, the personification of this type of architect has been Peter Zumthor, who coincidentally was awarded the Pritzker Prize only a few months after the beginning of the recession. Often viewed as a quasi-hermit, Zumthor produces architecture with an aura of abstinence. The most blatant example of this caricature of asceticism is his 2011 pavilion for the Serpentine Gallery, a temporary structure for one of the most exclusive sites in London: Kensington Gardens. Both through its name, 'Hortus Conclusus', and its arrangement, an open-air garden enclosed by a rectangular wooden gallery, the pavilion was immediately reminiscent of a monastery. One interesting formal aspect was the double enclosing wall with staggered entrances, which meant that visitors wishing to access the garden were forced to walk within the narrow and dark corridor between the two walls. This extremely ritualistic entrance was staged in order to amplify the experience of passing from the 'profane' outside to the 'sacred' inside. The pastoral setting of the park and the simplicity of the pavilion presented an aura of 'humility and redemption' in opposition to the profane restlessness of the city. And yet, as Andrea Phillips noted in a review, the pavilion's pretended humility was 'at odds with the speculative machinery of transnational architectural financing that the commission otherwise represents'.[33] She concluded that Zumthor's Pavilion was an 'austerity pavilion', representing what she called the 'pastoral politics' that capital has embraced in the wake of the recession. These pastoral politics operate by ideologically smothering growing economic and social inequality with images of contemplation and reconciliation with nature. Here asceticism loses its 'destructive character' and becomes an empty shell, whose emptiness is inversely proportional to the vast financial wealth that this kind of architecture represents.

However, there is a much more interesting example of this sort of asceticism, which summarises in a subtle way the discontents of minimal design. It is the photograph that portrays Steve Jobs, the founder of Apple, in the living room of his house in Los Gatos, California. Taken by Diana Walker in 1983, when Jobs was already a successful multi-millionaire entrepreneur, it shows him with a cup of tea in one hand, sitting on the floor in the middle of a conspicuously empty room furnished only with a lamp and a record player. There is a certain beauty about the photograph precisely because it does not look constructed, but conveys a sense of everyday life. At the same time it is not a casual situation either. Jobs sits at the centre of the photograph staring at the viewer as if the scene in which he is the main protagonist is a sort of declaration of intent. Commenting on the photograph, he said it was just the way he was living at that time: 'I was single, all you need is a cup of tea, a light and your stereo, you know, and that's what I had.' Compared to the glossy and over-designed minimalism of Pawson, or the mystical aura of Zumthor's 'humility', Jobs's asceticism looks more *real*, more genuine, and one must admit that here minimal design achieves one of its best ever performances. There is a striking resemblance to Hannes Meyer's Co-op Zimmer, though it is unlikely Jobs knew of the project. Indeed Jobs's room is even more drastic in reducing belongings to a bare minimum. As in Meyer's room, Jobs's extreme minimalism does not renounce the record player—its frugal sense of enjoyment becomes more important here than other gadgets that are usually considered more necessary (such as a telephone or TV). The photograph confirms that in his own way Jobs was an ascetic, and understood that his 'will to power' could only be strengthened through careful self-control. But Jobs's asceticism went beyond his living room in Los Gatos to become one of the most successful branding machines in the history of corporate capitalism. There is no space here to describe the obsession with simplicity that has characterised the design of Apple products. Perhaps it is more interesting to see how Jobs's ascetic design of himself became the centrepiece of Apple's success.

Like the abbot of a monastic order, Jobs imposed on his collaborators a strict discipline informed not only by a focus on work but also by frugality, as reflected in his desire to have all Apple workers clad in the same uniform. Jobs himself, like a monk, was an ascetic eater, and he always wore the same clothes—jeans and a black turtleneck—his own version of a monk's *habitus*. When he became mortally ill, his asceticism became more extreme. The illness did not disrupt his image of self-determination and concentration on the essential, but made this aspect of his life even stronger. All these aspects are concentrated and magnified in Walker's photograph, which gave Job's life a highly specific form, and I would argue this form is one of the most powerful statements about design and architecture of the last 30 years.

So what's wrong with Steve Jobs's asceticism? Apparently *nothing* is wrong. Asceticism is ultimately not about poverty or simplicity per se, but these aspects are among the possible means of this practice. And yet in Jobs's perfect asceticism there is indeed something fundamentally wrong, and it concerns the very purpose of asceticism. As we have seen, ascetic practice put a major emphasis on *how* we live. To be an ascetic means to be constantly in control of oneself, to be aware of one's body and one's mind and to train them constantly towards the goal of living according to one's own principles. Jobs's asceticism is in this sense a false asceticism—

not for the obvious reason that he made a lot of money, but because the form of life implied in what he helped to conceive and produce has nothing to do with *his own life*. Leaving aside the market-driven nature of Jobs's work, which would be too easy to criticise, it is the technology to which he devoted his ascetic life that has dramatically disrupted any possible control of one's self. I don't want to discuss the discontents of our digital age and end up with a luddite rant against smartphones, yet there is a fundamental problem with the digital age that people like Steve Jobs have helped to bring about: the dramatic shortage of attention.

If there is a *real* scarcity in the world (which the rhetoric of austerity does not mention at all), it is the scarcity of attention, which has now been consumed by a state of permanent distraction, driven by increasingly sophisticated means of communication and production. Actually distraction is not bad in itself. Within industrialisation, distraction in the form of idle talk, lack of focus, daydreaming, was a way in which subjects would be able to disconnect themselves from production and stay within themselves. But in a cognitive production in which every fraction of our life is put to work, distraction becomes a form of production, because it pushes people to do many things at the same time. While the capacity to focus on something for longer than five minutes is dramatically reduced, the compulsive dependence on the internet feeds the frantic production machinery of the web. Lack of focus is no longer caused by sloth, one of Christianity's deadly sins, but by a form of default Stakhanovism, which forces us to work more even when we don't work at all. While Jobs perfected his asceticism to rule himself (before strictly ruling others), the users of the devices he helped to spread are no longer able to control themselves.[34]

But there is something even more deeply disquieting about Jobs's photograph, which is precisely its spiritual aura, its pseudo-religious look, something that has subtly informed much of Apple's branding image and design, as well as Job's life. As with Pawson's boutique-religious minimalism, and Zumthor's aloofness, commercialism is here wrapped with an aura of restraint. This aura, this ideological need to balance market-saturation with pseudo-religious needs, is precisely the tendency that Benjamin saw as arising from the poverty of experience caused by the wealth of information and communication. As Benjamin wrote, 'With this tremendous development of technology a completely new poverty has descended on mankind. And the reverse of this poverty is the oppressive wealth that has been spread among people, or rather has swamped them entirely—ideas that have come with the revival of astrology, and the wisdom of yoga, Christian science and chiromancy, vegetarianism and gnosis, scholasticism and spirituality.'[35]

CHAPTER
VII

As we have seen, the perversion of asceticism is not simply its translation as 'austerity' but also its branding as image, which in times of austerity has become not only fashionable but also ideological. And yet it is precisely because economic austerity is a subjective economy, aiming to manipulate the subject's moral and ethical sphere, that asceticism offers also the possibility to emancipate subjectivity from such manipulation. If art and design play a fundamental role in amplifying the ideological overtones of austerity, they can also offer the clue to radical alternatives. As Hölderlin famously wrote, 'But where the danger is, also grows the saving power.' Within contemporary art there are several examples of artists who have understood how their life, even in its daily details, is an integral part of the artistic principles of their work.

Among them there is one artist in particular who has pushed this ascetic aspect of artistic production to an extreme, although his project has remained incomplete. I'm referring to the six prototypes for individual inhabitable spaces conceived by the Israeli artist Absalon between the late 1980s and 1993, the year in which he died of HIV at 28.[36] Absalon was raised in Ashdod and at an early age attended a military boarding school, which had a strong influence on his life. After finishing his military service, he decided to withdraw and live by the sea in a very small wooden hut that he had built himself. Dissatisfied with his life in Israel, he decided to move to Paris and become an artist. From the beginning, his work was very much focused on architecture. Apart from the six prototypes that he realised at 1:1 scale, his entire oeuvre consists of sculptures that resemble models of possible architectures. All realised in wood and painted white, the style of these models is decidedly minimalist. And yet their form was conceived not by the image, but more in terms of the possible life that would take place in them. An interesting feature of Absalon's work is a series of videos, such as *Solutions*, in which he filmed himself trying to inhabit one of his prototypes. In these videos it becomes clear how Absalon wanted to study human life in its tiny details, in order to understand what sort of space would be able to accommodate and eventually reform such a life. There is a strong connection between this aspect of his work and the architecture of the modern movement, where the goal was to reinvent architecture not only as a matter of style, but also as an enactment of a radically different form of life than the one implied by the nineteenth-century bourgeois interior. Of course this attempt to make architecture adhere to life, in the way that the concave adheres to the convex, is not an innocent operation. After all, Gropius collaborator and former Bauhaus student Ernst Neufert found it was a short step from perfecting a functional understanding of architecture in his *Architect's Data* to being appointed by Albert Speer to work on the standardisation of German industrial architecture. Absalon's prototypes are more reminiscent of Le Corbusier's architecture, in which the relationship between form and life is not just functional but challenging. Even though Le Corbusier made every effort to promote his architecture as liberating, his residential architecture is often deliberately demanding. Think of the extremely narrow spaces of the Unité d'Habitation, or the impossibly tight spaces of the monks' cells in the monastery of La Tourette. In the spaces that Le Corbusier designed for himself—such as the tiny *cabanon,* where all that is necessary for living is concentrated in a few square metres, or his personal room in his atelier in Rue de Sèvres, made so small that people would feel uncomfortable and cut meetings short—architecture does not simply accommodate specific domestic rituals but enacts them, without fully conditioning them. It is not by chance that Le Corbusier was heavily influenced by monasteries such as those of Mount Athos, where he spent three months, or Galluzzo, where as we have seen architecture is the clear diagram of daily life rituals. Abasalon himself went to live in architecture designed by Le Corbusier (Maison Lipchiz), and his forms are often literally reminiscent of the purism of Corb's early work. But unlike the Swiss architect, Absalon did not design his residential architecture for the masses: he insisted that these cells were conceived for himself and that he did not intend others to live in them.

Absalon's six small houses were conceived for different cities, the places where he would have to travel for work. In fact, just before his untimely death, he decided that he would spend the rest of his days in these cells, making his life and not just his designed objects a *work of art*. What is left of this project are the prototypes, which today are exhibited inside museums and galleries as art-objects, betraying their meaning. Here we see the fundamental aspect of asceticism, which is a practice that is always centred on the self and not something that should be imposed on others.

Each house was designed by Absalon according to his own body, and was thus large enough to be inhabited himself and the occasional visitor. He wanted these spaces to limit his possessions to almost nothing and to reduce domestic maintenance to the minimum. All the necessary equipment for living was supposed to be built into the walls of the structures. Yet these houses were not designed to be functional or easily inhabited. On the contrary, Absalon intended them to impose a very strict discipline on his existence. They would force him not only to possess the bare minimum, but also to live alone and to develop a form of life radically different from the social norm (couple, family). Absalon viewed these houses as a radical act of self-enactment centred not on what has become the fetish of consumerist culture—desire—but on its opposite, restraint. And yet he understood restraint not as a punitive discipline but as a way to give form to his chosen way of life. Here his project shows us something decisive about self-organisation: namely, the increased importance of rules and form. Contrary to the easy romanticism of self-organisation that is so popular among architects and designers, it requires a lot of effort and self-discipline to exit a pre-existing social order. Presenting the concept of these houses in a lecture, Absalon affirmed: 'I can't imagine a life without structure, I'm sure that I have to create new rules to escape from other rules. It is a kind of technique of living. Inventing new rules, constraints, despite the fact that it can be restrictive, creating one's own constraints, I think that is the best way, I can't imagine any other way.'[37]

It is interesting to note that Absalon did not want his projects to be understood as a utopian gesture. He affirmed several times that he had no interest in addressing any broader social programme. His only goal was to change his own life, consciously. Unlike many artists and designers, he focused on his own life as the ultimate form of his own work.

And yet by projecting this radical self-enactment Absalon pointed to a way to act that has been largely overlooked in contemporary art and design. Today many artists, architects and designers feel the urge to promote social change through their proposals, but they rarely look at their own existence, which is what really constitutes the main source of their production. Many people working in the field of architecture, art and design live in very precarious conditions, doing unpaid work and having no social security. Their lives are increasingly characterised by anxiety, anguish, frustration, and sometimes depression. In spite of the socially minded agenda that curators, architects and artists eagerly endorse in their initiatives, we know that the field of the creative industries is highly competitive and has no mercy for those who refuse to stay in tune with it. And yet these creative workers have difficulty admitting this reality, and because the field is so competitive, it seems almost impossible for them to organise themselves within something like a union or a social organisation that would protect them from exploitation. Ironically, many of these people already live an ascetic life, but unwillingly, without being capable of giving this life a more autonomous structure, a structure that would enable them, like the early monks, to live according to their own idiorrhythmy, rather than the frantic schedules of post-fordist modes of production. Within this condition the slogan 'less is more' appears, at best, a sarcastic commentary on our increasingly precarious condition, because we now know that less is just less and there is very little about it that can still be romanticised. At the same time it is precisely in creative work, where the boundary between work and non-work is impossible to trace, that life itself has become the main source of production (and exploitation)—and this should be seen as the opportunity to focus on *ars vivendi* as a fundamental form of resistance. The legacy of ascetic practices should be understood as giving us the means to change the status quo by focusing on our lives—or better, to see our lives in all their material and organisational aspects as a possibility for change.

There is something fundamentally schizo-phrenic about neoliberal forms of governance, which pair cuts to welfare and social protection with measures to stimulate individual consumption. This paradox is fully visible in the world of design. On the one hand we see the rise of socially oriented design, where the virtue is to do 'more with less' and where scarcity of resources is enthusiasti-cally celebrated as the trigger for creativity, while on the other hand design stubbornly continues to focus on value-free innovation, on inventing expensive useless gadgets justified solely by the pretence that this production helps the design industry to survive. So capitalists tell us that the only way we can counter the recession is to invest more in possessions at the same time as we are deprived of the most basic social welfare. In the face of this scenario, asceticism is perhaps an ironic stance, because it not only gives us a proper picture of our condition, but also makes it possible for us to redefine what is really necessary and what is not, outside the regime of scarcity imposed by the market. Asceticism is thus the possibility of reclaiming a *good life* and with it the hope that we can live—and live better—with less. However this *less* should not be transformed into an ideology: less is *not* more, less is just less. Only when we are able to reach beyond its ideological aura, can less be the starting point for an alternative form of life that is independent of both the false needs imposed by the market and the austerity policies imposed by debt. To say less is enough is to refuse the moral blackmail of the debt economy, which threatens us on the basis of our own expectations of greater wealth. While economy can only assess social wealth in terms of *more* – that is, more development and more growth—to say *less is enough* is an attempt to define a way of living that is beyond both the promise of growth and the threatening rhetoric of scarcity. But this way of living has to be developed, not through the wishful thinking of utopian visions, but by focusing on *us,* by trying to redefine our lives starting from the most basic daily routines. Such an ascetic focus may be indispensable if we really want to try to live together with others.

There is an increasing interest in more socially oriented ways of living such as co-housing or sharing domestic space beyond the compound of the family apartment. But what is seldom discussed is that this way of life requires some effort. To live together requires less individual freedom, although that may be no bad thing. The question is whether such a way of life might only be developed out of economic necessity, or because it is only by sharing and coexisting that we can reclaim the true subjectivity that Marx beautifully described with the oxymoron 'social individuals'—individuals who only become so among other individuals. Here, less means precisely the recalibration of a form of reciprocity that is no longer driven by possession but by sharing; the less we have in terms of possessions, the more we'll be able to share. To say *enough* (instead of more) means to redefine what we really need in order to live a good life—that is, a life detached from the social ethos of property, from the anxiety of production and possession, and where less is just enough.

END NOTES

1   'Less is More' comes from Robert Browning's poem 'Andrea del Sarto', and was used by Mies in reference to restraint in an interview in the *New York Herald Tribune* on 28 June 1959.

2   For an interesting critique of how architects have responded to economic austerity by simply translating it into a formal aesthetic see: Jeremy Till, 'Scarcity Contra Austerity' in 'Places', last retrieved July 2003, places.designobserver.com/feature/scarcity-contra-austerity/35638/.

3   There are many examples of overnight volte-faces after the 2008 crisis, but the most blatant was a piece written by the then architecture critic for the *New York Times*, Nicolai Ourousoff, significantly titled 'It Was Fun Till the Money Ran Out'. After years of celebrating starachitects' conquest of the world, Ourousoff concluded his 2008 with praise for more socially oriented architecture. See *New York Times*, 19 December 2008.

4   As in the case of Rem Koolhaas and his office OMA. Just a month after the beginning of the economic crisis, OMA associate Renier De Graaf launched a manifesto called 'Simplicity' where the proposal for a seven-star high-rise hotel in Dubai designed as a simple monolith was presented as an architecture against the spectacle of iconic buildings. See Renier De Graaf, 'Simplicity' in Hans Ulrich Obrist (ed), *Manifesto Marathon, Serpentine Gallery* (Cologne: Walther Koenig, 2013), 28.

5   See Nishat Awan, Tatjana Schneider, Jeremy Till, *Spatial Agency: Other Ways of Doing Architecture* (London: Routledge, 2011).

6   Stefano Boeri, *Fare di più con meno* (Milan: Il Saggiatore 2012).

7   For an interesting philosophical enquiry on the concept of industry and its role within human creativity see Gerald Raunig, *Factories of Knowledge, Industries of Creativity* (Los Angeles: Semiotext(e), 2013), 111–22.

8   See Elettra Stimilli, *Il debito del vivente* (Macerata: Quodlibet, 2011).

9   See Maurizio Lazzarato, *The Making of Indebted Man* (Los Angeles: Semiotext(e), 2012), 31.

10   Max Weber, *Protestant Ethics and the Spirit of Capitalism* (London: Penguin, 2002 [1905]).

11   See Sven-Olow Wallenstein, *Architecture and Biopolitcs* (New York: Princeton Architectural Press, FORuM Project, 2008).

12   See Elettra Stimilli, 'Il Carattere Distruttivo dell'Ascetismo', in Seminario di Studi Benjaminiani (ed), *Le Vie della distruzione: a partire dal* Il carattere distruttivo *di Walter Benjamin* (Macerata: Quodlibet, 2010), 123–42.

13   See JWC Wand, *A History of the Early Church to AD 500* (London: Routledge 1994).

14   The Church's attitude towards hermitic life was ambivalent. On the one hand the extreme asceticism practised by hermits offered a very charismatic example of Christian life, especially in those places that shared borders with other religions, such as Islam in the Middle East. At the same time the Catholic Church feared extreme forms of life that questioned the social role that the Church assumed within the Empire.

15   See Samuel Angus, *The Environment of Early Christianity* (New York: Charles Scribner, 1917).

16   See Friedrich Nietzsche, *Zur Genealogie der Moral*, in *Werke*, VI: 2 (Berlin: Gruyter, 1968).

17   Roland Barthes, *How To Live Together: Novelistic Simulations of some Everyday Spaces* (New York: Columbia University Press, 2013).

18   On the institution of the rule see Candido Mazon, *Las reglas de los religiosos. Su obligacion y naturaleza juridica* (Rome: Pontificia Università Gregoriana, 1940); see also Giorgio Agamben, *Altissima Povertà. Regole monastiche e forme di vita* (Vicenza: Neri Pozza, 2012).

19   See Richard Gilyard-Beer, *Abbeys: The Religious Houses of England and Wales* (London: Her Majesty's Stationery Office, 1958).

20   For a reading of the monastery as a progenitor of the industrial organisation of society see James Madge, 'Monasticism and the Culture of Production' in *Issue* 3, July 1982, 1–4.

21   On this see the fundamental reading of the monastic rule made by Giorgio Agamben in his book *Altissima Povertà*, op cit note 18.

22   Agamben, *Altissima Povertà,* 151–75.

END NOTES

23   Sebastiano Serlio, *On Domestic Architecture* (London: Dover, 1996).

24   One of the most accurate and interesting discussions of Le Corbusier's Maison Dom-Ino is in Adolf Max Vogt, *Le Corbusier, The Noble Savage* (Cambridge, MA: MIT Press, 2000).

25   Among these essays the most notable are: 'Experience and Poverty', and 'Moscow'. See *Walter Benjamin: Selected Writings, Volume 2, part 2, 1931–1934*, ed Michael W Jennings et al, trans Rodney Livingstone (Cambridge, MA: Belknap Press of Harvard University Press, 1999).

26   Ibid, 731–36.

27   Ibid, 732.

28   Ibid, 541.

29   Ibid, 541.

30   Ibid, 22–46.

31   On the Co-op Zimmer see 'Hilde Heynen, Leaving Traces: Anonimity in the Modern House' in Penny Sparke, Anne Massey, Trevor Keeble, Brendan Martin (eds), *Designing the Modern Interior* (Oxford: Berg, 2009), 123.

32   The Unknown Hipster, John Pawson's Monastery in Novy Dvur, retrieved July 2013, www.unknownhipster. com/2012/04/12/john-pawsons-monastery-of-novy-dvur/

33   Andrea Phillips, 'English Pastoral', in *Log* 23 (Fall 2011), 81.

34   Jobs himself told his biographer Walter Isaacson how his interest in Zen meditation taught him to ignore distractions and to cultivate concentration, the very thing that has been destroyed by the technology he helped to implement. See Walter Isaacson, *Steve Jobs* (New York: Simon and Schuster, 2011).

35   Walter Benjamin, 'Experience and Poverty', in *Walter Benjamin: Selected Writings, Volume 2, part 2, 1931–1934*, 732.

36   See Susanne Pfeffer (ed), *Absalon* (Cologne: Walther Koenig, 2012).

37   Ibid, 265.

ACKNOWLEDGEMENTS

I am deeply grateful to Justin McGuirk for his very useful critical feedback and editorial suggestions. Many thanks also to Maria S Giudici for having discussed the themes developed here.

THE ACTION IS THE FORM
VICTOR HUGO'S TED TALK
BY KELLER EASTERLING

ACROSS THE PLAZA
THE PUBLIC VOIDS OF THE
POST-SOVIET CITY
BY OWEN HATHERLEY

EDGE CITY
DRIVING THE PERIPHERY OF SÃO PAULO
BY JUSTIN MCGUIRK

LESS IS ENOUGH
ON ARCHITECTURE AND ASCETICISM
BY PIER VITTORIO AURELI

ISBN 978-0-9929146-0-8

Printed and bound by Printondemand-Worldwide
Published by Strelka Press

First edition.

The typeface used within this book is called Lazurski, it was designed
at the Soviet type design bureau, Polygraphmash, by Vladimir Yefimov
in 1984. It is a homage to a 1960s font designed by Vadim Lazurski
that was inspired by Italian typefaces of the early 16th century.

WS - #0099 - 150823 - C0 - 179/111/6 - PB - 9780992914608 - Gloss Lamination